Write Now

*Elementary guided composition
through pictures and puzzles*

Ronald Ridout

Illustrated by Sally Kindberg

Longman

LONGMAN GROUP UK LIMITED
Longman House, Burnt Mill, Harlow,
Essex CM20 2JE, England
and Associated Companies throughout the world

First published 1975
Twelfth impression 1990

ISBN 0-582-55220-6

Filmset by Keyspools Ltd, Golborne, Lancs

Produced by Longman Singapore Publishers Pte Ltd
Printed in Singapore

To the teacher

Even the writing of single sentences could legitimately have come under the very large umbrella 'composition'. But a line had to be drawn somewhere and, as the aim is ultimately to guide the student in writing connected sentences—in composing descriptions, accounts, letters, explanations, instructions, narratives, articles, memoranda, records—I have restricted my use of the word to putting two or more sentences together on paper.

The word 'guided' calls for definition too. Guidance can be given in a variety of ways, including the traditional talk or rules about writing. The guidance I have to offer in this little book has almost nothing to do with academic lecturing about composition, and everything to do with guiding the student into writing sentences with a meaningful content, sensibly linked together, correctly constructed, and acceptably worded, so that in the process of doing so he will gain an insight into the particular problem of writing English and will gradually build up the habit of correct or acceptable composition in English.

Composition without such guidance—free composition—leads to the student making innumerable mistakes, since he inevitably tries to express himself in structural items he has not yet mastered. It is not only unsuccessful, it actually does him harm. To produce effective results he must be guided into using the structures he has already learnt, and using them correctly. Guiding the student thus into writing correct English before he can do so unaided is now universally understood to be the only useful sort of composition the teacher can undertake during the first few years of teaching a foreign language. The principle has been accepted, but its implementation has been impeded by the lack of material for teaching in this way.

Up till now the teacher has had access to books of composition, in which the student is given the complete story in the form of pictures and has only to clothe it in words. Such books have been popular and up to a point useful, since they have at least given the student something definite to write about. But unfortunately it is in the actual writing that the learner of a foreign language needs most guidance and this is not easy to provide with the picture approach, though suitable vocabulary can be suggested and an appropriate structure may be referred to. Its usefulness as guidance has been exploited and developed in the present book, but it is in any case only one possible approach and quite insufficient on its own.

Another widely used device for getting the student to write correct compositions is to ask a number of questions about a description, a picture, a story, an explanation, the answers to which add up to a composition in its own right. Guidance of this kind has been made use of in this book. But it is severely limited by its artificiality. The questions have to be answered in a manner that would not be normal in a straightforward question and answer exchange, in order to gain the continuity demanded by the composition. Moreover, it is doubtful whether many students gain much insight into the problem of composition in this way, since the sentences arrive on his paper quite independently of the process of writing connected sentences. In other words, there is minimal transfer from this activity to that of writing in general.

That still leaves us with many other devices for guiding the learner to write correctly. Some of them have been employed elsewhere and some may be familiar in another context, but as an integrated and structurally graded course in composition they are entirely new. They include the following:

1   A description of a picture is given as a guide for writing a similar description of another picture which is so devised that the main features are exactly similar, thus calling for the use of the same kind of language structures. Sometimes the vocabulary is contained in the originating material, as in 2, 15. Sometimes the new vocabulary is listed, as in 1, 48.

2   A description or account about someone else is given as a guide for the student to adapt to his own circumstances. This may be fairly tightly controlled, as in 1(3), 23, 29, 36, or it may be more open-ended as in 53, 70, 75.

3   A simple dialogue of 6–10 lines is given as a close model. The circumstances are changed slightly and the student has to rewrite the dialogue to fit the new circumstances, as in 3, 7. When the changes are more far-reaching, as in 43, the rewriting becomes more difficult.

4   Continuous dialogues can also be written from substitution frames (e.g. 10, 33, 35, 47). With the right control, this is less mechanical than it sounds, since the items cannot be chosen without understanding.

5 The symbol language of number can be translated into continuous sentences (4, 12, 37, 87), once the model has been set.

6 A variety of tabulated information (5, 32, 38, 41, 53, 56) can be converted into continuous sentences to be used as a model for further conversions, the content being thus provided and the language structure prescribed.

7 Games (11) can be used as a model for rather more open-ended dialogue writing than in 1.

8 The re-ordering of sentences to tell a story can be used to give a better-understood model for story writing. This can be done with the help of pictures, (15(A), 19, 59) or without their help (15(C)).

9 A more open-ended development of 6 is to give the pictures and some vocabulary and ask the pupil to tell the story (19(B), 67).

10 Much more guided is the story told from pictures on the basis of answers to questions about the pictures (18, 26, 27, 30, 60, 83, 86). The student is told how to convert his answers into real narrative.

11 Students can be guided into writing instructions for performing certain operations by being given a description of the process and shown how to convert these descriptions into instructions (21).

12 Giving instructions can also be guided by the use of street plans (45, 81).

13 TV commentaries can be used as a guide for writing similar commentaries to fit another set of TV pictures as in 20

14 Maps may be used as a variation of the tabulated information of 4, as in 34, 36.

15 Writing riddles to the models given (40, 84) is a possible motivation, and can exercise a variety of tenses.

16 Solving word puzzles (55, 65, 66, 80) can provide the motivation for describing a meaningful activity.

17 The solving of verbal problems (63, 68, 71, 88, 89, 90) can likewise lead to writing an account of something done personally, the language resources being found in the verbalisation of the problem itself.

18 Calendars and clocks can be used for guiding a few connected sentences about dates and times that bring an insight into the expression of time (76, 78).

Such a variety of approach is itself valuable in maintaining interest, but it also prevents the one-track mind and so keeps the student alert, facilitates his insight into the problem and thus maximises the transfer of what he is learning to the writing of English in general.

Whether the book is useful or not also depends on its grading. If the main language problem being dealt with is the use of those structures involved by the present continuous tense, the student's time will be largely wasted if he is also required to handle the present perfect tense, which he hasn't yet been taught. This will not be much hindrance to those students using this book as a general revision course, since they will already be reasonably familiar with the more advanced structure, but it will be a serious obstacle to those using the book with only a year or less of English learning behind them. To make it as workable as possible for beginners, I have presupposed no knowledge of the language beyond the new structures and those that have already been practised. This makes the book usable at a much earlier stage than would otherwise be possible. The first seven compositions for example, can be written entirely within the limits of the present tense of the verb 'to be' and may thus be tackled within the first few months or even weeks of starting the language.

The fact that any of the structures already practised may be drawn upon means that the earlier ones are constantly being revised. Moreover, whenever there is a large combination of earlier structures, the student not only consolidates previous work, but also writes to the full limits of his effective knowledge of the language; he is approaching 'real' composition.

Grading in terms of the construction of the composition is less important. Clearly at the elementary stage we are not concerned with the construction of multi-paragraph compositions; that would come only at an advanced stage. At the same time, just because the student has completed a longish paragraph on page 16 there is no reason why he should not be asked to write a mere two or three sentences much later on. In the context of more difficult language, this simple two-sentence composition may well be valid practice in its own right; it will certainly be valid as preparation for the lengthier composition that follows.

It will be seen from this description that the guidance always consists of help in avoiding mistakes and therefore in writing acceptable English. The method is essentially one of self-help. Everywhere, by one means or another the book enables the student to help himself to write, and to write without mistakes, what he would not otherwise be able to do. For only in this way will he learn to write; by making mistakes, as is inevitable in free composition, he will learn little more than the mistakes he makes.

He cannot, however, write in a vacuum. He must have a situation in which to write. So much is this so, that some recent guided composition books have been called situational composition. This places the emphasis on content, whereas with a foreign language, essential though content is, the main problem is writing good English. With the emphasis on situation, guidance with the actual writing tends to be neglected. In the present book the guidance covers both situation and language, but the situation is merely made to serve the purpose of writing good English.

The situation is always clearly defined. In many instances there is a model piece of writing arising out of a situation. The student is then required to imitate this writing by writing sentences to fit the same type of situation with minor changes in it. He is thus supplied with the number of sentences required, the kind of sentences required, the structural elements to use, and in most cases all the vocabulary required to meet the modified situation; he is enabled to help himself to write with the minimum likelihood of mistakes.

R.R.

This is a man. His name is Tom Green. His shirt is white, and his trousers are grey. His trousers are very big, and his nose is very big too. (It is not his real nose.) Tom Green is a clown. He is on a tight rope. The rope is in the circus.

This is a lady. Her name is Rosemary Taylor. Her dress is white and her shoes are black. Her dress is pretty, and her face is pretty too. Rosemary Taylor is an actress. She is on the stage. The stage is in the theatre.

Now write similar sentences about:
1 Richard Jackson   2 Jane Brown
Here are some useful words:

  farmer   long   skirt   hair   tractor
  teacher   short   blouse   school   field

Tom Green is speaking:
I am a man. My name is Tom Green. My shirt is white and my trousers are . . . .
3 Finish Tom Green's sentences.
4 Write the sentences for Rosemary Taylor.
5 Now write similar sentences for yourself.
   This is what Bob wrote:
I am a boy. My name is Bob Smith. My shirt is white and my trousers are grey. My shoes are big, and my feet are big too. (They are my feet!) I am a student. I am at my desk. My desk is in the classroom.

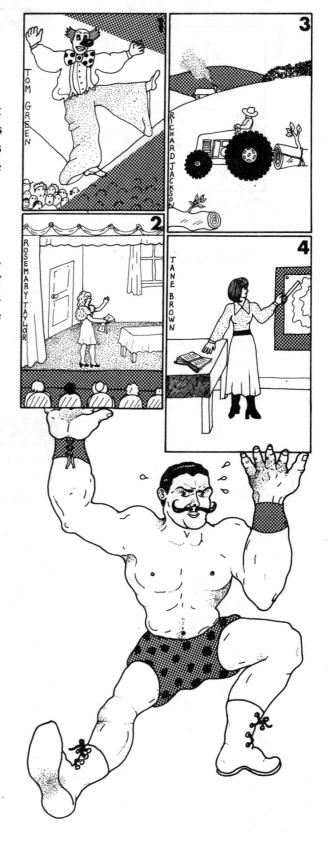

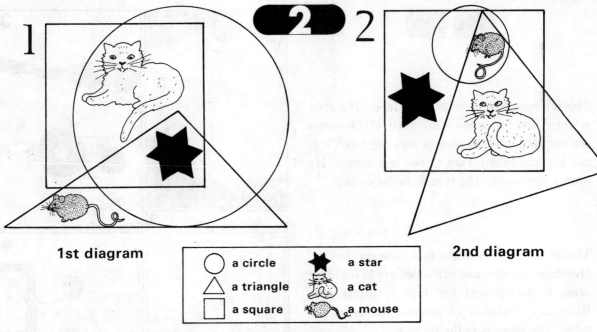

1st diagram

○ a circle		★ a star	
△ a triangle		🐱 a cat	
□ a square		🐭 a mouse	

2nd diagram

In the first diagram the star is in the circle, the square and the triangle. The cat is in the circle and the square. The mouse is in only the triangle.

Now write three similar sentences about the second diagram.

3

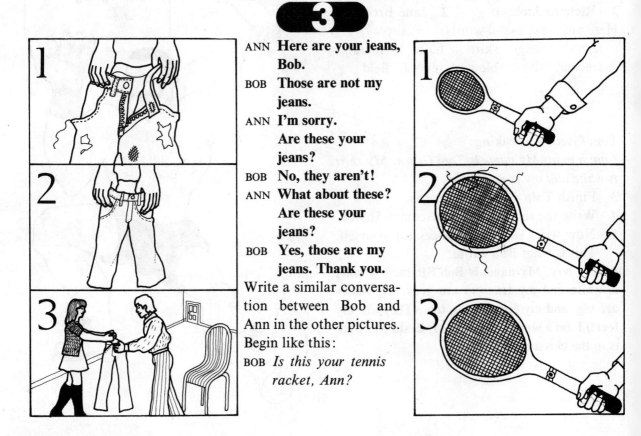

ANN **Here are your jeans, Bob.**

BOB **Those are not my jeans.**

ANN **I'm sorry. Are these your jeans?**

BOB **No, they aren't!**

ANN **What about these? Are these your jeans?**

BOB **Yes, those are my jeans. Thank you.**

Write a similar conversation between Bob and Ann in the other pictures. Begin like this:

BOB *Is this your tennis racket, Ann?*

This is an addition sum. Can you add in English? This is what you say:

Two and nine are eleven. Eleven and seven are eighteen. Eighteen and three are twenty-one. Twenty-one and six are twenty-seven. The answer is twenty-seven.

Now add up these sums. Write five sentences for each sum.

NAME	NATIONALITY	BROTHER	SISTER	CLASS	NUMBER IN CLASS	POSITION OF DESK
Pedro Cervantes	Spanish	Miguel	Elena	2	33	Second row
Anneke Kuipers	Dutch	Henk	—	1A	29	Front row
Manuel Correia	Brazilian	—	Maria	2B	30	Back row
Ilsa Schwartz	German	Franz	—	2	28	Third row

Pedro wrote this:

My name is Pedro Cervantes. I am Spanish. My brother's name is Miguel, and my sister's name is Elena. I am in Class 2. There are 33 pupils in our class. My desk is in the second row.

Now write six similar sentences for:

        1 Anneke   **2** Manuel   **3** Ilsa

4 Now write five sentences *about* Anneke. Begin like this: *Anneke Kuipers is Dutch. Her . . .*

6

John is not a good painter. This is his picture. It is a picture of a big bird. No, it isn't. It's a picture of a plane. That is the nose. Those are the wings, and those are the wheels. The plane is on the ground. It is a white plane.

Ann is a good painter. This is her picture. It is a picture of a horse. That is the head, and that is the tail. Those are the legs. The horse is in a field. It is a grey horse.

Now write similar sentences about: **1** Bob's picture **2** Jill's picture

7

A Whose car is that?
B Which one?
A The one in front of your Mini.
B Oh, that's Mr Wood's Fiat.
A It's very old, isn't it?
B Yes, it's a 1960 model.

Write another conversation between **A** and **B**. Begin:
A *Whose bicycle is that?*
(It's David's bicycle and it's by the lamp-post. It's a 1959 model.)

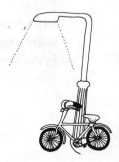

4

8 I can see some stars at the top of the first blackboard.
I can see some circles at the bottom. I can see some letters on the left side, and I can see some squares on the right. I can see a plane in the middle.
Now say what you can see on the second blackboard. Write four sentences.

9

What can Bob see? What can he see on the road, in the field, on the gate, in the sky, on the sea, on the beach? Begin like this: *Bob can see some cars on the road. He can . . .*

A		
I can't see	the jet plane. the helicopter. the small planes.	

B		
It is They are	over there. to your right. to your left.	

A		
Is it Are they	in the air? on the ground?	

B		
No,	it isn't. they aren't.	

A		
Where	is it, are they,	then?

B		
It is They are	in the air. on the ground.	

A		
Oh, yes, I can see	it them	now.

Here is one conversation between **A** and **B**:

A I can't see the jet plane.
B It is to your right.
A Is it on the ground?
B No it isn't.
A Where is it then?
B It is in the air.
A Oh, yes, I can see it now.

Now write two more conversations. Look at the pictures carefully. Then choose from the frames.

11

This is a game.
Bob is a donkey, but he doesn't know this.
He wants to find out what he is.
He is asking questions:

BOB	**Can I climb trees, Ann?**
ANN	**No, you can't.**
BOB	**Can I fly, David?**
DAVID	**No, you can't.**
BOB	**Can I walk on four legs, Jill?**
JILL	**Yes, you can.**
BOB	**Are my ears very long, Peter?**
PETER	**Yes, they are.**
BOB	**Can I say 'Ee-aw, Clare?**
CLARE	**Yes, you can.**
BOB	**Am I a donkey?**
ALL	**Yes, you are!**

1 Play the game again. Ann is a cat (or cow). Let the children ask similar questions. Write out the questions and answers.

2 Play the game once more. Peter is a duck (or owl). Write out the questions and answers.

12

This is a multiplication sum.
It is wrong. The correct answer is 48.
Twice three is six.
Six times four is twenty-four.
Twenty-four times two is forty-eight.

This is an addition sum.
It is wrong. The correct answer is 78.
Fifteen and six are twenty-one.
Twenty-one and ten are thirty-one.
Thirty-one and forty-seven are seventy-eight.

Write about the sums **A**, **B**, **C** and **D** in the same way.

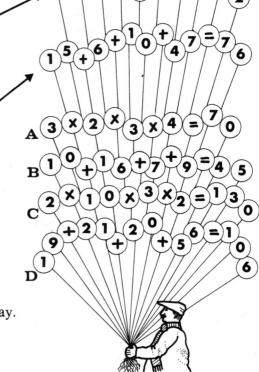

13

Here are five boys in a row. They are watching a football match. David is in the middle of the row. Bob is sitting on David's left, and Sam is sitting on Bob's left. Peter is standing between Richard and David.

1 Can you give each boy his right name?
2 These girls are watching a netball match. Write a similar description of them in four sentences.

MARY   JILL

LIZ   SUE   LINDA

14

PETER   JILL   BOB   CLARE   DAVID   ANN   JOHN

Peter is chasing Jill, and Jill is chasing Bob. Clare is chasing David, and David is chasing Ann. Ann is chasing John, and John is chasing the dog. The dog is running away with their picnic basket.

Now write four sentences about the picture on the left.

CAT

TOM

MRS HUNT

FARMER'S WIFE

FARMER'S SON

HEN   FOX   DOG   THE FARMER

8

15

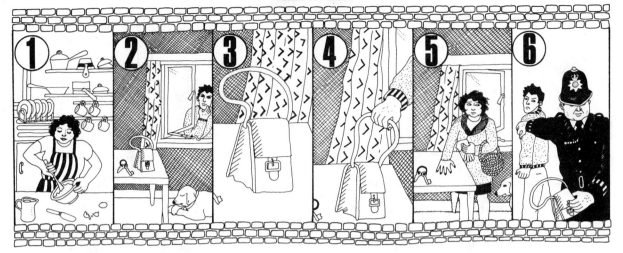

A What is happening in the pictures? These sentences tell you. Write them in their right order.

> A man is standing at the window. He is looking at the bag.
>
> Mrs King can't find her bag, and so she can't go shopping.
>
> The bag is on the table in the dining room.
>
> Now everything is all right. A policeman is bringing back the bag.
>
> Mrs King is cooking in the kitchen.
>
> Now he is in the dining room. He is taking the bag.

B Here is another story. Can you put the sentences in their right order? There is only one picture this time.

> The chocolate cake is all over Jill's clothes.
>
> Now Jill is walking into Ann—crash!
>
> Ann is carrying a very big chocolate cake.
>
> It is all over Ann's clothes too.
>
> Her friend Jill is reading a book.
>
> Ann is walking towards Jill, and Jill is walking towards Ann.

C Can you put the sentences of this story in their right order too? There are no pictures this time.

> Now he is climbing up the tree.
>
> Now he is falling off the branch.
>
> Tommy is walking towards a big tree.
>
> Now he is walking along the branch. His hands are in the air.
>
> He is lying on the ground now.
>
> He is standing on a high branch.

16

1 It is quarter to eight. Bob is getting up.

He is putting on his shirt.

What is Bob doing in the other pictures? Write three similar sentences about each picture. You may need these words:

having	boiled egg	waving	desk
breakfast	school	talking	classroom
eating	saying	pupils	lesson

17

Bob, Ann and their dog are on the beach.

They are not swimming or diving now.

They are having a picnic.

Ann is drinking a cup of coffee.

Bob is eating an icecream.

The dog is drinking some water.

Write out two possible conversations between **A** and **B** using the information given above.

A

| I can't see | Bob.
Ann.
the dog. | Is | she
it
he | diving?
swimming? |

B

| No, | he
she
it | is not | diving.
swimming. |

A

| What is | he
she
it | doing, then? |

B

| He
She
It | is | drinking.
eating. |

A

| What is | he
she
it | eating?
drinking? |

B

| He
She
It | is | eating
drinking | a cup of coffee.
an icecream.
some water. |

A Write the answers to these questions:

1. The man in the picture is Mr Bull. Where is Mr Bull?
2. Is he awake or asleep?
3. The boy in the second picture is Bob. What is he doing now?
4. Where are the apples falling?
5. Look at the fourth picture. Is Mr Bull awake or asleep now?
6. Is he pleased or angry?
7. What is Bob doing?
8. What is Mr Bull doing in the fifth picture?
9. Where is Bob in the sixth picture?
10. What is Mr Bull doing to him?
11. Is Bob sad in the last picture?
12. Where is he going?

B Look at your answers to the questions. They tell the story of the pictures. But they are not continuous. Rewrite them in the form of a continuous story.

ANSWERS

1 *He is under the apple tree.*
2 *He is asleep.*
3 *He is shaking the tree.*

STORY

Mr Bull is under an apple tree.
He is asleep. Bob is shaking the tree now . . .

A What is happening in the pictures? These sentences tell you. Write them in the same order as the pictures.

Now the boy is running away from the bull.
Now the boy is jumping over the gate.
In this picture a boy is walking across a field.
The bull is very near the boy now, but the boy is climbing over the gate.
At last the bull is on one side of the gate and the boy is safe on the other side.
In the next picture the bull is running towards the boy.

B Now tell the story of these pictures. What is happening in each? Begin like this: *In this picture a boy is flying his kite.*

tree	fetching	climbing up	hand
getting	ladder	climbing down	again

1 Tom Wilson has the ball. He is running along the left wing.
2 Now he is passing the ball to Bob Jones.
3 Bob Jones is running down the centre with the ball at his feet, but a defender is coming towards him.
4 Now Bob Jones is past the defender. There is only the goalkeeper in front of him.
5 Bob Jones is shooting. It's a good shot. The goalkeeper is ready for it.

6 But he can't stop it. The ball is in the net. It's a goal!

Describe what is happening in each of the pictures below. Begin like this:

1 *Bob Jones has the ball, but a defender is coming towards him.*
2 *Bob Jones is passing the ball . . .*

1 Bob Jones
2 to Jack Smith
3 right wing
4 into the centre
5 Bob Jones heading
6 saving

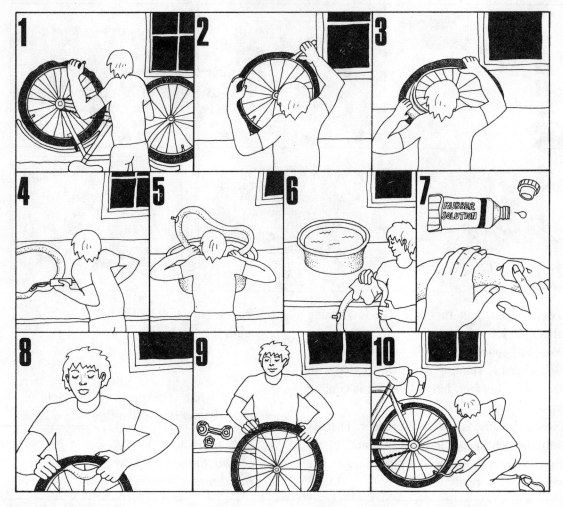

A Bob is mending a puncture. Write the sentences in their correct order.

Now he is putting on the tyre and putting the wheel back on the bicycle.

Now he is putting some air in the tube.

Last of all he is blowing up the tyre.

Now he is sticking a patch over the hole.

Bob is turning his bicycle upside-down.

Now he is putting the tube in the water and finding the hole.

Now he is putting the tube back.

Now he is taking out the tube.

Now he is drying the tube.

Now he is taking off the wheel, and then the tyre.

B How do you mend a puncture?
Give the instructions in ten sentences, like this:

First turn your bicycle upside-down.
Then take off . . .
Next . . .
Then . . .
After that . . .
Next . . .
Then . . .
After that . . .
Then . . .
Last of all . . .

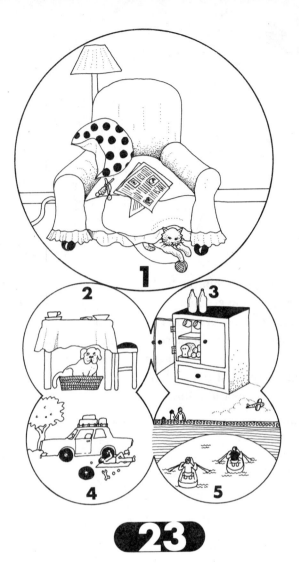

1 I can see an armchair in the first picture.
There is a cushion, a newspaper and some knitting on the armchair.
There is a kitten under it, and there is a reading lamp behind it.

Now write three similar sentences about each of the other pictures. You may need these words:

dog	food	roof	tree	bridge
basket	bottles	luggage	children	rowing
saucer	shelf	tools	watching	plane

Bob is speaking:

There are twenty-five desks in my classroom. My desk is in the third row. There are four desks on my right and there are two in front of me and two behind me. There aren't any desks to my left, because I am sitting by the wall. But there is a window on my left, and there is a window on my right. Tom is sitting in front of me, and Clare is sitting behind me. Jill is sitting on my right. Our teacher is standing in front of us at the moment. He is holding a book in his left hand.

Now write nine or ten sentences like these, but make them true for *you*.

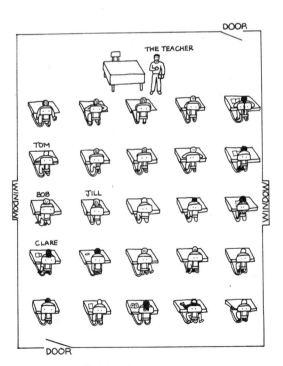

Bob's classroom

There are two groups of children in the pictures above. There are seven children in the group on the left. All the children in this group are girls. They are holding hands and dancing in a ring. In the group on the right there are eight children. They are not in a ring. They are walking in a line. The children at the front are girls, and those at the back are boys. They are marching into school in a line.

Make a similar description of the picture on the left and below.

25

In the first picture there is a man in the garden. He is picking apples. He is putting them in a big box. There are already a lot of apples in the box. There is someone in the house too. It is a girl. She is standing at the door. She is watching the man. There is a puppy in her arms.

Now write about the second picture in the same way.

1 Look at the first picture. Is there a boy or a girl on the bridge?
2 What is he doing?
3 Look at the second picture. Is he walking on the wall now, or is he falling off?
4 What is there under the bridge in the third picture?
5 Where is the boy falling?
6 Look at the last picture. Where is the boy now?
7 How many people are there in the plane now?

Look at your seven answers. They tell the story of the pictures. But the sentences are not quite right. Make them completely right, e.g.

ANSWERS	*STORY*
1 *There is a boy on the bridge.*	*There is a boy on the bridge in the first picture. He is walking along the wall. . . .*
2 *He is walking along the wall.*	

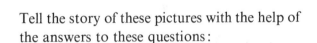

Tell the story of these pictures with the help of the answers to these questions:

1 Who is there on the wall?
  What is he picking?
  Is he stealing them?
  Who is there at the window?
  Is he watching the boy?
2 Is the man talking to his dog now?
  Is the door open or shut?
3 Who is the dog barking at?
  Is the boy frightened?
4 Is the dog chasing the boy now?
  Where is the basket of apples now?

There are two trucks in the first picture. There is someone in the big truck. It is the driver. He is sitting at the driving wheel. There is nothing in the back of the truck. It is empty. But there is something in the small truck. It is full of bags of cement. No one is sitting at the driving wheel. The front of the truck is empty. The driver is under the truck. He is mending something.

Now write a similar description of the second picture.

My name is Pedro Gonzalez. There are five people in my family. I have a mother, a father and two sisters, but I haven't any brothers. My father is an engineer. My sisters are at the primary school and I am at the secondary school. I am at school now. I am sitting at my desk. There is an exercise book on my desk and I am writing some English sentences in it. There are 30 pupils in my class. So there are 30 exercise books on 30 desks, and 30 pupils are writing in the 30 exercise books!

Write similar sentences, but make them true for you.

Can you answer these questions about the picture?

1 Are there many people on this beach?
2 Are they all sitting in deck chairs?
3 Are some sitting on the sand?
4 Is the little girl covering her mother or her father with sand?
5 Is the little boy pouring water over his sister or his brother?
6 What is the fat man doing?
7 Is the fat lady eating an icecream?
8 How many sailing boats are there on the sea?
9 Is there a raft on the sea too?
10 How many people are there on the raft?
11 How many are diving into the sea?
12 How many are swimming to the beach?

Now describe the picture. Begin like this:
This is a picture of the seaside. There are a lot of people on the beach. Some of them are sitting in deck chairs, and . . .

This is a picture of the Brown family. Mr Brown is the father. Mrs Brown is the mother. Their children are John, Jill and May. So Mr and Mrs Brown have a son and two daughters. John has two sisters, Jill and May. Jill has a sister and a brother. John is standing between his sisters. The three children are standing in front of their parents.

Now write eight similar sentences about the Smith family.

FIRST NAME	SURNAME	NATIONALITY	AGE	COLOUR OF HAIR	BROTHERS	SISTERS	FATHER'S JOB
Alberto	Correia	Brazilian	12	brown	0	1	doctor
Maria	Bianchi	Italian	11	dark	1	0	singer
Shizuo	Matsuo	Japanese	12	black	0	1	engineer
Ann	Smith	British	13	fair	0	0	bank clerk
Chuma	Ojo	Nigerian	11	black	1	1	teacher

My first name is Alberto and my surname is Correia. I am Brazilian. I am twelve years old and have brown hair. I have a sister but no brother. My father is a doctor.

What do the others say? Write five sentences for each.

Now write five sentences *about* each child, like this:
The second child's first name is Maria and her surname is Bianchi. She is Italian . . .

A

Where is	Robert? David? Mary? Susan?

B

He She	is	standing over there. talking to the others. under the tree.

A

Is	he she	the girl with the fair hair? the boy with the very long hair? the girl in jeans? the boy in shorts?

B

No,	he she	has short hair. is wearing a dress. is wearing long trousers. has dark hair.

A

Oh,	I can see that's now I can see	her. him.

Write out two possible conversations between **A** and **B**, like this:

A **Where is Mary?**
B **She is talking to the others.**
A **Is she the girl in jeans?**
B **No, she is wearing a dress.**
A **Oh, now I can see her.**

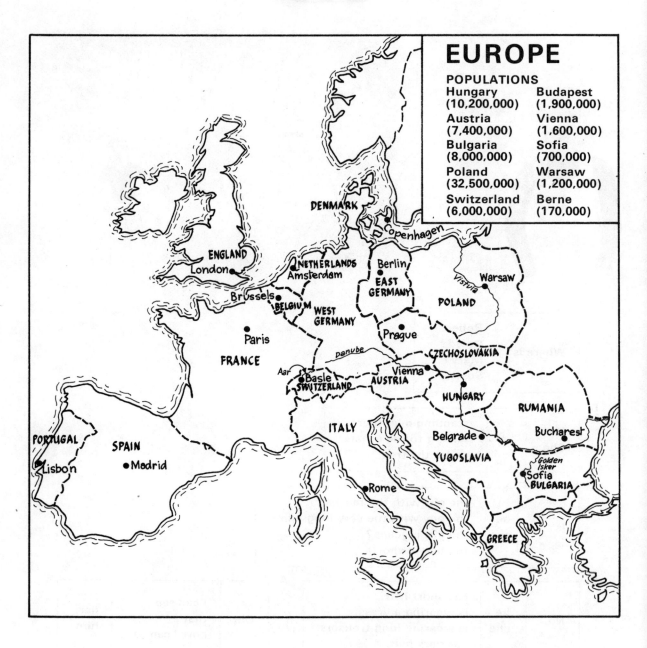

EUROPE

POPULATIONS

Hungary (10,200,000)	Budapest (1,900,000)
Austria (7,400,000)	Vienna (1,600,000)
Bulgaria (8,000,000)	Sofia (700,000)
Poland (32,500,000)	Warsaw (1,200,000)
Switzerland (6,000,000)	Berne (170,000)

Hungary is between Austria and Rumania. Czechoslovakia is to the north, and Yugoslavia is to the south. There are 10,200,000 people in Hungary. The capital of Hungary is Budapest. It is on the river Danube, and has a population of 1,900,000.

Now write four similar sentences about:

1 Austria   3 Poland
2 Bulgaria   4 Switzerland

BOB   SUSAN   PETER   JILL

Look at the pictures and then make up three more conversations like this from the frames:

A   **Is anyone pumping anything up in the pictures?**
B   **Yes, Peter is pumping something up in the third picture.**
A   **What is he pumping up?**
B   **He is pumping up his bicycle tyre.**

Is anyone	pumping pulling sweeping hanging	anything	up	in the pictures ?

Yes,	Bob Susan Peter Jill	is	pumping pulling sweeping hanging	something	up	in the	first second third last	picture.

What is	he she	pumping pulling sweeping hanging	up?

He She	is	pumping pulling sweeping hanging	up	a picture. some pieces of paper. his bicycle tyre. a very large weed.

23

36

Her name is Roberta, and she comes from Italy.
She lives in Genoa.
She speaks Italian at home, but she is learning English at school.

A Now write three similar sentences about each of these children. Their languages are Spanish, French, Japanese, Portuguese.

B Miguel is writing:
My name is Miguel and I come from Spain.
I live in Madrid. I speak Spanish at home, but I am learning English at school.
Write three similar sentences for Roberta, Collette, Tatsuo and Maria.

C Now write three similar sentences about yourself.

24

Fourteen plus six equals twenty.

Twenty plus fifty-three equals seventy-three.

Seventy-three plus twenty-eight equals a hundred and one.

Fifteen minus nine equals six.

Six plus forty-six equals fifty-two.

Fifty-two minus thirty-five equals seventeen.

Now write out the sums **A, B, C, D** and **E** in the same way.

38

NAME	HOME	GETS UP	OCCUPATION	STARTS WORK	RETURNS HOME
Mr Brown	England	7.45	shopkeeper	9.00	6.00
Mr Johnson	Canada	7.30	teacher	9.00	4.30
Mr Cook	Australia	7.15	printer	8.30	5.30
Mr Wang	Hong Kong	7.00	engineer	8.00	5.15
Mr Ojo	Nigeria	6.00	clerk	7.30	4.00

Mr Brown lives in England. He gets up at quarter to eight every morning. He is a shopkeeper. He starts work at nine and returns home at six o'clock.

Now write four similar sentences about:

1 Mr Johnson   **2** Mr Cook   **3** Mr Wang   **4** Mr Ojo

5 Now Mr Brown is writing. He begins like this: *My name is Henry Brown, and I live in England.* Finish it for him.

39

A Who is the boy in jeans?
B Oh, that's Pedro.
A Where does Pedro come from?
B He comes from Buenos Aires.
A What language does he speak, then?
B He speaks Spanish. They speak Spanish in Argentina.
A Yes, of course they do. How silly of me!

Write another conversation like this between **A** and **B**, about a girl in slacks. Her name is Maria and she comes from São Paulo in Brazil. She speaks Portuguese of course.

40

A It has a long tail and lives in trees. It eats nuts and bananas. What is it? (It's a monkey.)
B It is yellow and round. The earth goes round it. It gives us light and warmth. What is it? (It's the sun.)
C It is a bird. The first letter of its name is D, and the last is K. It swims on rivers and ponds. What is it? (It's a duck.)
D She works in a hospital. The first letter of her name is N, and the middle letter is R. What is she? (She is a nurse.)
E It has four legs and a back, but it can't walk or bend. What is it? (It's a chair.)

These are riddles for young children. Make up some more riddles for young children. Make up one about each of these:

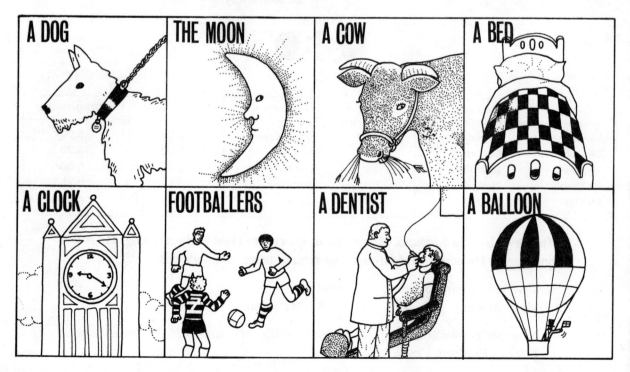

A DOG   THE MOON   A COW   A BED

A CLOCK   FOOTBALLERS   A DENTIST   A BALLOON

	JOHN PARSONS	ISABEL HUNT
Age	11	12
Address	15 High Street, Bristol	72 Bridge Road, Leeds
School	Somton Comprehensive School	West End Secondary School
Head Teacher	Mr James Brown	Mrs Ann Lake
Class	IB	IIc
Height	5 ft. 2 in.	5 ft. 4 in.
Weight	108 lb.	106 lb.
Build	Broad	Slim
Games	Favourite: football also cricket	Favourite: tennis also hockey
Other Activities	Likes swimming and cycling	Likes riding ponies
		Can play the piano

John Parsons is eleven years old and lives at 15 High Street, Bristol. He attends Somton Comprehensive School. His Head Teacher's name is Mr James Brown, and he is in class IB. John is broad in build, is 5 ft. 2 in. tall and weighs 108 lb. His favourite game is football, but he also plays cricket. He likes swimming and cycling.

A Write a similar description of Isabel Hunt.

B Now write a similar description of yourself.

My name is Jill Brown. I live at Number 21 Park Road. Our neighbours on one side are the Smiths. Those on the other side are the Morgans. So we live between the Smiths and the Morgans. The Cooks live opposite us. The Greens live in the house on their left, and the Taylors live in the house on their right.

Now write seven similar sentences for Sam Taylor. He lives at Number 18 Park Road.

A Does this bus go to the airport?
B No, it's going in the opposite direction.
A Where do I catch a bus for the airport, then?
B They stop over there on the other side of the road.
A Oh, I see, just outside the cinema.
B Yes, that's right.

Write similar conversations between a child and a bus conductor. Begin like this:

1 *Is this the right bus for the city centre?* (It only goes to the station. Buses for the centre stop down the road by the post office.)

2 *Are you going to the beach?* (The bus is going to the sports centre. Buses for the beach stop in the square, outside the town hall.)

3 *Does this bus take me to the swimming pool?* (It is going to the airport. Buses for the swimming pool stop up the street by the bridge.)

This list is in alphabetical order.

arm	The word *arm* comes before *back*, because a comes before b.
back	The word *back* comes before *bed*, because a comes before e.
bed	The word *bed* comes before *bell*, because d comes before l.
bell	The word *bell* comes before *belt*, because l comes before t.
belt	

Now write four similar sentences about each of these alphabetical lists:

1	part	**2**	Henry	**3**	race	**4**	clear	**5**	train
	rare		Jack		sack		dark		shop
	real		Jean		seat		deaf		start
	red		Joan		send		deep		stone
	rest		John		sent		deer		stop

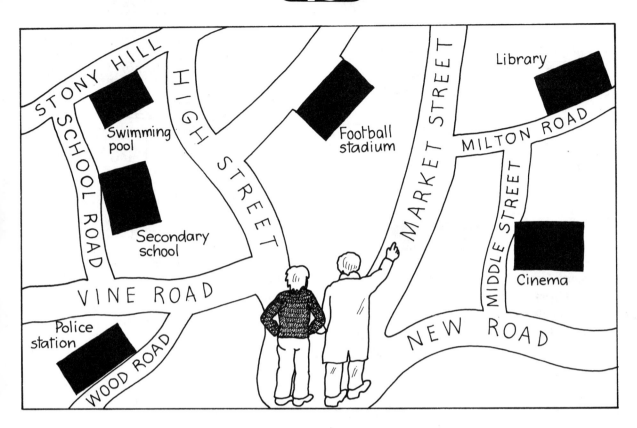

BOB	Excuse me. How do I get to the library, please?
A STRANGER	You go up Market Street and take the first turning on the right. That brings you into Milton Road. The library is a little way along on the left.
BOB	Is it very far?
STRANGER	No, it's only four or five hundred yards. You can walk there in about five minutes.
BOB	Thank you so much.

Write five similar conversations between a child and a stranger. The child is standing in the square. This is the first line of each conversation:

1 SUSAN Excuse me. Can you tell me the way to the cinema, please?
2 TOM   Excuse me. Which way do I go for the football stadium, please?
3 MARY   Excuse me. How do I get to the swimming pool, please?
4 DAVID Excuse me. What is the way to the secondary school, please?
5 CLARE Excuse me. How do I get to the police station, please?

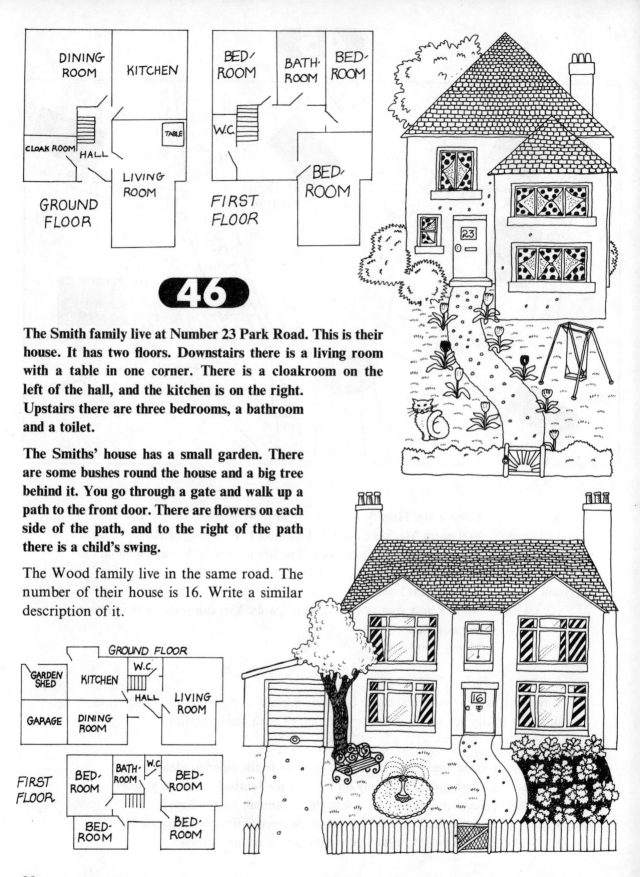

46

The Smith family live at Number 23 Park Road. This is their house. It has two floors. Downstairs there is a living room with a table in one corner. There is a cloakroom on the left of the hall, and the kitchen is on the right. Upstairs there are three bedrooms, a bathroom and a toilet.

The Smiths' house has a small garden. There are some bushes round the house and a big tree behind it. You go through a gate and walk up a path to the front door. There are flowers on each side of the path, and to the right of the path there is a child's swing.

The Wood family live in the same road. The number of their house is 16. Write a similar description of it.

Write out four conversations between A and B.

A

What is	Bob Ann Jill Peter	looking for? wearing? getting? borrowing?

B

He She	is	looking for wearing getting borrowing	a racket. her swim suit. a pair of scissors. a basket.

A

Why is	he she	looking for wearing getting borrowing	a racket? her swim suit? a pair of scissors? a basket?

B

He She	is going to	play tennis with David. have a swim. cut his toe nails. cut out a dress for her young sister. do the shopping for old Mrs Larkins.

What are they going to do? Add two sentences, like this:

1 **Susan is standing at the edge of the swimming pool.**
She is going to dive in.
Then she is going to swim to the other side.

Here are some useful words:

climb	put on	wash	read
clean	river	dry	write
draw	catch	get out	exercise

1 Susan is standing at the edge of the swim-ming pool.
2 Bob is walking towards the ladder.
3 Jill is opening her English book.
4 The teacher is picking up the duster.
5 Ann is taking her new blouse from the cupboard.
6 Mr Hill is getting his fishing rod.
7 Tom is turning on the tap.
8 Richard is swimming towards the side of the pool.

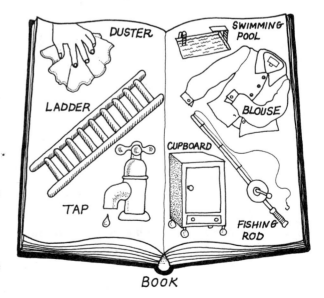

DUSTER
SWIMMING POOL
LADDER
BLOUSE
CUPBOARD
TAP
FISHING ROD
BOOK

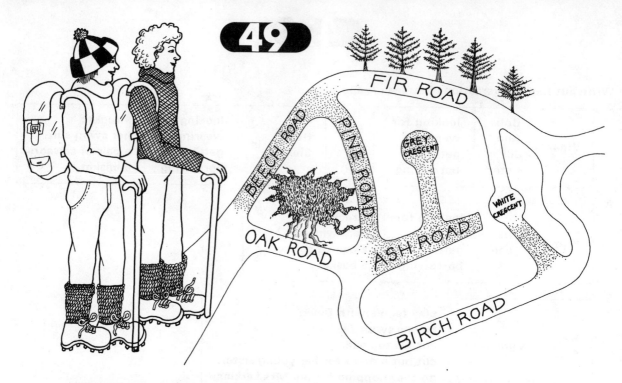

Mr White can only travel on white roads, and Mr Grey can only travel on grey roads. How is Mr White going to walk to White Crescent, and how is Mr Grey going to walk to Grey Crescent?

Mr Grey can't take Oak Road because it is white; so he is going to walk along Beech Road. At the end of Beech Road he can't take Fir Road because it is white; so he is going to walk along Pine Road. At the end of Pine Road he can't take Birch Road because it is white; so he is going to walk along Ash Road. Half way along Ash Road he is going to turn to the left into Grey Crescent.

Now explain how Mr White is going to reach White Crescent.

Mrs Pink is going to unlock the cupboard. She is going to do it with that key. Then she is going to take out some silver dishes.

Now say how the following people are going to do the things, and what they are going to do afterwards.

1   **Mr Brown is going to sharpen his pencil.**
2   **Mrs White is going to sweep the floor.**
3   **Mr Black is going to open a bottle of wine.**
4   **Mr Grey is going to cut that piece of wood.**
5   **Mr Green is going to dig his garden.**
6   **Mr Blue is going to wash his car.**

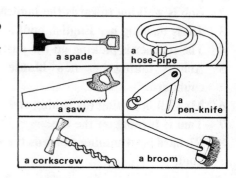

a spade
a hose-pipe
a saw
a pen-knife
a corkscrew
a broom

Write out four conversations between **A** and **B**. Check with the pictures.

A

Did	Bob Ann Peter Clare	go to visit	the circus the cinema the football match the museum	on Sunday ?

B

No,	he she	went to visited	her aunt's house. his uncle's farm. the seaside.

A

Did	he she	have	a swim a ride a picnic a walk	there ?

B

Yes, No,	he she	did. didn't.

BOB

ANN

PETER

CLARE

The teacher is speaking, but it is now the next day.

What did the children do? Begin like this:

1 *Peter gave John a piece of paper.*
Then he showed the teacher his work.

1 Give John a piece of paper, Peter. Then show me your work.
2 Draw the car, Charles. Then give it its correct name.
3 Write your name on the envelope, John. Then give it to me.
4 Give Ann a book, Bob. Then finish the exercise.
5 Show George the photo, Michael. Then shut the door, please.
6 Give me your exercise book, Mary. Then show Clare your map.
7 Take Miss Brown the duster, Ann. Then come and see me.
8 Give Susan the small box, David. Then take the big one to Mr Jones in the next room.

53

	TOM		ANN
7.30	Wakes up	7.15	Wakes up
7.45	Gets up	7.30	Gets up
8.00	Begins breakfast	7.45	Begins breakfast
8.30	Goes to school on foot	8.30	Goes to school by bus
8.50	Arrives at school	8.45	Arrives at school
9.00	First lesson begins	9.00	First lesson begins
12.30	Lunch begins	12.30	Lunch begins
2.00	Afternoon school begins	2.00	Afternoon school begins
4.00	School finishes	4.00	School finishes
4.30	Gets home	4.15	Gets home

A   Tom normally wakes up at half past seven, and gets up at quarter to eight. He begins his breakfast at eight o'clock. At half past eight he goes to school on foot. He arrives there at ten to nine. The first lesson begins at nine o'clock. He begins his lunch at half past twelve. Afternoon school begins at two o'clock and finishes at four o'clock. Tom gets home at half past four.
Now write a similar paragraph about Ann.

B   Yesterday Ann woke up at quarter past seven, and got up at half past seven. She began breakfast at quarter to eight. At half past eight she went to school by bus. She arrived there at quarter to nine. Her first lesson began at nine o'clock. She began her lunch at half past twelve. Afternoon school began at two o'clock and finished at four o'clock. Ann got home at quarter past four.
Now write a similar paragraph about what Tom did yesterday.

C   Write a similar paragraph about what you did yesterday.

Complete this story. Put the word for the picture.

1 Yesterday Peter crossed a over a river.

2 There was a small on the bridge.

3 Suddenly he fell into the .

4 Peter took off his and jumped into the water.

5 He to the little boy.

6 He held the little boy with one and then swam to the edge of the river.

7 The next day the boy's called at Peter's house.

8 He thanked Peter for saving his son's life and gave him a new pop .

Let Peter tell the story. Begin like this: *Yesterday I crossed a bridge . . .*
Now let the little boy tell the story. Begin like this: *Yesterday I was on a . . .*

55

There are two words in each group of letters. The second word is the opposite of the first. Cross out the letters of the first word and leave the letters of the second word. Here is an example:

Ł H Į E A Ǥ V Y Ħ Ṭ

Solve the six puzzles. Then say what you did each time, like this:

I crossed out the letters L-I-G-H-T. In this way I left the letters H-E-A-V-Y. Heavy is the opposite of light.

56

This table means that John Brown married Mary White. They had three children, Christine, Susan and Paul. Susan married Simon Grey. They called their two children David and Peter. Paul married Jane Pink and they called their children Arthur and Clare. Christine did not marry.

Now explain what this table means:

John Brown — Mary White

Christine   Susan   Simon Grey   Paul   Jane Pink

David   Peter   Arthur   Clare

Michael Baker — Kate Farmer

Richard   Nicola Buck   Roger Mason   Helen

Robert   Joyce   Ann   Elizabeth   Isabel

57

Bob is playing football with Peter in this picture. Their goal is two trees. Bob is the goalkeeper, and Peter is kicking the ball to him. But the ball is not going into the goal. It is going into the branches of the tree on Bob's right.

This happened and finished yesterday. Bob is writing about it. What does he write? Begin like this: *I played football with Peter yesterday. Our goal was . . .*

BOY   LORRY   MINI SCOOTER VAN ROLLS-ROYCE

Can you write these sentences in their correct order?

A scooter put on its brakes and pulled up behind that.
A lorry put on its brakes and pulled up just in time.
There was a very rich fat old man in the Rolls.
A little boy walked across the busy road.
A van put on its brakes and pulled up behind that.
A Mini put on its brakes and pulled up behind the lorry.
The ash from his large cigar fell all over his trousers.
A Rolls Royce put on its brakes and pulled up behind that.

Now write eight similar sentences about this picture. The fat lady in the Jaguar had a drink in her hand.

DOG VAN SCOOTER   AUSTIN   LORRY   JAGUAR

These sentences tell the story of the pictures, but they are in the wrong order.
Write them in the correct order.

The tiger charged the hunter.

The hunter got up and shut the door.

The hunter saw a tiger and was very frightened.

The hunter was very near his hut. He tripped over a stone.

He turned round and ran away.

The tiger ran over him and went into the hut.

Now write the story of the pictures below. The answers to the questions will help you.

1   **Who crawled to the bird cage?**
2   **Did he climb on to a chair? What did he do then?**
3   **What flew out of the cage? Where did it fly?**
4   **Who saw the bird in the garden?**
5   **Did Bob catch it in his hands or in a net?**
6   **Where did he take the bird? Did he shut the door?**

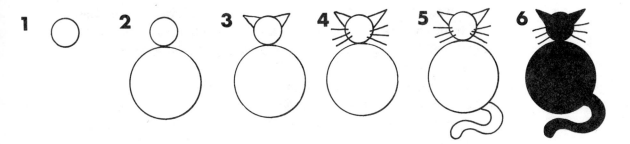

Susan is speaking:

1 **Watch me. I am going to draw a small circle.**
2 **Now I am going to draw a big circle under the small one.**
3 **Now I am going to draw ears on the small circle.**
4 **·Now I am going to draw whiskers on it.**
5 **Now I am going to draw a tail on the big circle.**
6 **Last of all I am going to make everything black.**

A   In the six sentences above, Susan is speaking before she draws. She is now speaking while she is drawing. What is she saying? Begin like this:

  1 *Watch me. I am drawing a small circle. . . .*

B   Susan finished the cat. She then said what she did. What did she say? Write like this:

  First I drew a small circle. Then I. . . . Then. . . . Then. . . . Then. . . . Last of all. . . .

62

A   It is now the next Sunday. Susan wrote down what she did each day of the week before. What did she write? She began like this: *On Sunday I visited Grandma . . .*

B   It is the Saturday before. Susan is still going to do these things. Write down what she is going to do. Begin: *On Sunday I am going to visit Grandma . . .*

C   Write down what *you* did each day last week.

3 SUN	*Visit grandma*
4 MON	*Buy a film for the camera*
5 TUE	*Watch play on T.V.*
6 WED	*Clean my bicycle*
7 THUR	*Wash my hair*
8 FRI	*Buy a present for Bob's birthday*
9 SAT	*See the new James Bond film at the ODEON*

a Two boys, Tom and Jack, and their father and uncle want to cross a river. They have a small boat. The boat can only carry 80 kilograms. After that it sinks! Tom and Jack each weigh 40 kg. Their father and uncle each weigh 80 kg. How did they all cross the river?

Here is the beginning of the answer. Can you finish it?

Tom and Jack crossed first. Tom stayed there and Jack brought back the boat. Then their father crossed alone. Tom brought back the boat. Then Tom and Jack crossed together. . . .

b **Here is a similar problem. Three men and two boys came to a deep river. There is a small boat. The boat can only carry two boys or one boy and a man. After that it sinks! How did the three men and two boys all cross the river? Begin your answer like this:** *The two boys crossed first. . . .*

Take a piece of chalk, Pedro.
Go to the blackboard.
Draw a box with a lid.
Give the picture a title.
Then give Alberto the chalk.

A BOX WITH A LID

Now Maria, tell us what Pedro did.

He took a piece of chalk. Then he went to the blackboard. After that he drew a box with a lid. Then he gave the picture a title. Last of all, he gave Alberto the chalk.

Now write down what these children did.

1 **Go to the window, Roberta. Open it. Look outside. Shut the window. Then go back to your seat.**

2 **Take out your book Miguel. Find page 22. Read the first question. Write down the answer. Then show me your paper.**

3 **Take your chair to the cupboard, Franz. Stand on it. Take two bottles from the top shelf. Give Ilsa one of the bottles. Then give me the other.**

4 **Go into the garden Isabel. Pick some flowers. Put them in the tall vase. Put the vase of flowers on the table. Then throw away the old flowers.**

s	w	a	n
w	i	p	e
a	p	e	s
n	e	s	t

CLUES

1 A large white bird with a long neck.
2 To dry with a cloth.
3 Large monkeys.
4 A bird's home.

This is a word square. You write the answers to the clues *across* the puzzle. The same words then appear *down* the puzzle. This is how you solve the puzzle. A large white bird with a long neck is a swan, so you begin at No 1, and write SWAN across the puzzle. To dry with a cloth is to wipe, so you begin at No 2 and write WIPE. Large monkeys are apes, so you begin at No 3 and write APES. Finally a bird's home is a nest, so you begin at No 4 and write NEST.

a Now write down very quickly what you did. Begin like this: *A large white bird with a long neck is a swan, so I began at No 1 and wrote . . .*

CLUES

1 Not fast.
2 To have a home (in, at).
3 A place to cook in.
4 The past tense of 'go'.

b Solve this word square. Then say what you did.

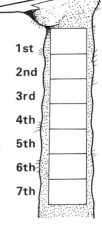

Can you solve this puzzle? The letters spell the name of a bird.

There is R in the middle. The letter I comes just below R. The last letter is H. C comes between I and H. The letter at the top is O. There is only one T, and it comes before R. There is an S between O and T.

How did you solve it? Write down what you did and why. Begin like this: *I wrote R in the fourth square because that is the middle one. I wrote I . . . because . . .*

1st
2nd
3rd
4th
5th
6th
7th

a Tell the story of this silly boy. Say what is happening in the pictures. Begin like this:

In the first picture Tom is carrying a saw.
In the second he is climbing up a tree.
In the third . . .

You need these words:

sitting	cutting	lying
branch	falling off	ground

b Tell the story again. It happened last week. Begin like this:

Last week Tom fetched a saw. Then he climbed up . . .

One day Bob wanted two litres of water. But he only had two cans. One can held five litres and the other held three litres. How did he get the two litres?

He filled the big can with water. Then he filled the small can from the big can. This left two litres in the big can.

The next day Bob wanted one litre of water. He still only had two cans. One held five litres and the other held three litres. How did he get the one litre? Begin your answer like this:

He filled the small can. Then he poured all the water into the big can. . . .

Bob is writing:

On Monday morning our first lesson is Geography.
On Tuesday morning we have Physics in our first lesson.
On Wednesday morning we have English first.
On Thursday morning our first lesson is Art.
On Friday morning we have Mathematics in the first lesson.

1   Now you are writing. Begin like this: *On Monday morning Bob's first lesson is Geography. . . .*

2   Now write five similar sentences about your timetable. Here are the names of other subjects: History, Physical Education, Chemistry, Biology, Science, Botany, Woodwork, Craft, Metal Work, Algebra, Arithmetic, Geometry, Latin.

3   It is now Sunday. Write five sentences about Bob's timetable last week. Begin like this: *On Monday morning last week Bob's first lesson was Geography. . . .*

Pedro came home from school at half past four yesterday. It was a hot day. His mother gave him a glass of cold water, and then he washed his hands. After that he sat down and did his homework. He finished it at six o'clock. He had dinner at half past six. Then he played with his friend from next door till bedtime. He read for about twenty minutes in bed and put his light out at half past nine.

Repeat the sentences, but make them true for you. Begin like this:

I came home from school at . . .

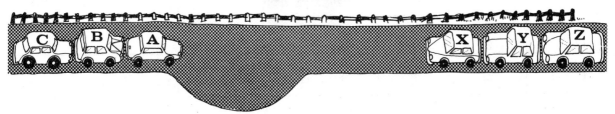

This is a very narrow road. One car cannot pass another car. But there is one wide part of the road. Here two cars can pass. How did the three cars X, Y, Z pass the three cars A, B, and C?

Car X drove into the wide part of the road. Cars A, B and C drove past the wide part and stopped at Car Y. Car X then drove out of the wide part and went on its way. Then cars ABC reversed past the wide part. . . .

72

Here is a sentence about each person in the pictures:

1 **Tommy is lying on the ground.**
2 **Pedro is sitting up and yawning.**
3 **Isabel is smelling some flowers.**
4 **Ann is looking at the broken pieces.**
5 **The goalkeeper has the ball in his hands.**
6 **Bob is pulling a fish out of the water.**

What have they just done, and what are they going to do? Add two sentences to each. Make up your sentences for Nos 5 and 6. Choose the others from these lists:

He has just woken up.
She has just dropped a dish.
He has just fallen off his bicycle.
She has just picked them.

She is going to put them in a vase soon.
He is going to stand up in a moment.
He is going to dress in a moment.
She is going to sweep up the bits in a moment.

TEAM	PLAYED	WON	LOST	DRAWN	GOALS		POINTS
					FOR	AGAINST	
Lions	4	2	0	2	10	5	6
City	3	1	0	2	6	4	4
Tigers	3	0	0	3	3	3	3
United	4	0	3	1	0	6	1

These four football teams play in a small league. This is the league table at the end of the first month. What have Lions done?

Lions have played four matches. They have won two of them and drawn two. They haven't lost any matches yet. They have scored ten goals and their opponents have scored five. They have won six points and are in the first position.

What have the other teams done? Write similar sentences about each of them.

44

Write out five different conversations between **A** and **B**.

A

Oh dear, what have you	dropped ? broken ? damaged ? lost ?

B

I have	dropped broken damaged lost	some money. my leg. some plates.	Have you	dropped broken damaged lost	anything	this morning ? today ? this week ?

A

No, I haven't	dropped broken damaged lost	anything	this morning. today. this week.

B

You are lucky ! You have all the luck ! Lucky you !

A

Well, the	morning day week	hasn't finished yet ! isn't over yet !

John has already done many things today. He has of course done the usual routine things: he has got up, washed, dressed, had breakfast and so on. But he has also done a number of special things. He has read the newspaper, he has tightened the brakes of his bicycle. He has ridden into town and bought a new football. He has washed and polished the car for his father. He has played his new pop record and he has written in his diary.

1 Let John say what he has already done today, like this:
   I have already done a number of special things today. I have . . .
2 Now write some similar sentences and say what *you* have already done today.

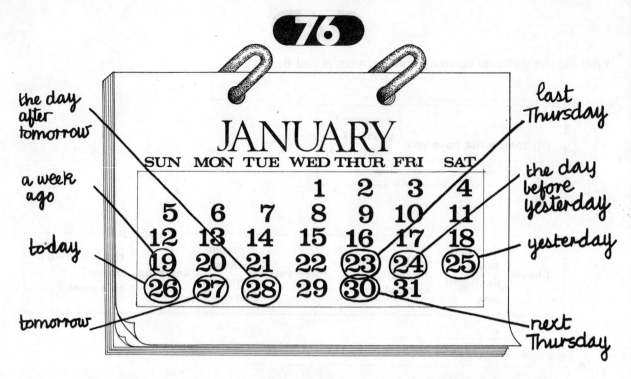

It is 26th January today. It was 25th January yesterday, and it will be 27th January tomorrow. It was 24th January the day before yesterday, and it will be 28th January the day after tomorrow. It was 23rd January last Thursday, and it will be 30th January next Thursday. It was 19th January a week ago, and it will be 2nd February in a week's time.

Now write five similar sentences about the dates in this calendar:

NAME	AGE NOW	BIRTHDAY
Susan	14	1st December
Bob	12	14th February
Jill	10	23rd July

NAME	AGE	BIRTHDAY
John	15	20th July
Ann	13	3rd March
Richard	12	22nd August

Susan is still 14. She will be 15 on 1st December. Her brother Bob is 12. He will be 13 on 14th February. Her sister Jill is only 10. She will be 11 on 23rd July.

Now look at the other table. Ann is John's sister and Richard is his brother. Write six similar sentences about them.

78

It is ten past six now.
It was twenty to six half an hour ago.
It will be twenty to seven in half an hour's time.

Now write three similar sentences for each of these:

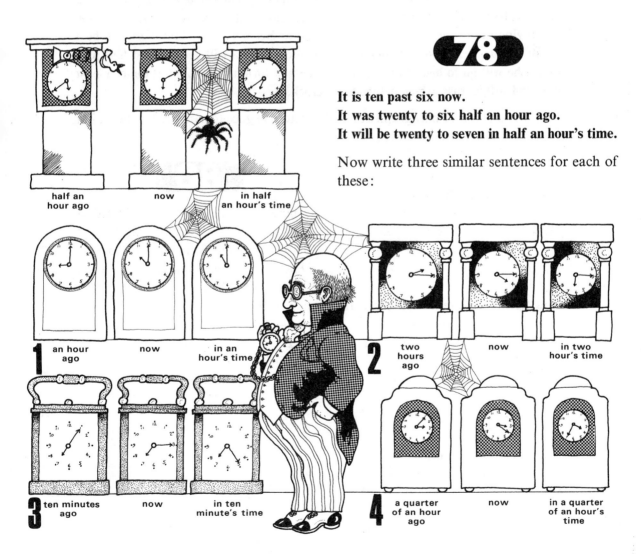

half an hour ago   now   in half an hour's time

1 an hour ago   now   in an hour's time

2 two hours ago   now   in two hour's time

3 ten minutes ago   now   in ten minute's time

4 a quarter of an hour ago   now   in a quarter of an hour's time

MARIA		ROBERTO	
7.30	Gets up	7.00	Gets up
8.45	Arrives at school	8.30	Arrives at school
9.00	First Lesson: History	8.45	First Lesson: Mathematics
9.45	Mathematics	9.30	Geography
10.30	Break	10.15	Break
10.45	English	10.30	Science
11.30	Science	11.15	English
12.15	Lunch	12.00	Lunch
4.00	Last lesson ends	3.45	School ends
4.30	Gets home	4.15	Gets home
9.00	Goes to bed	9.15	Goes to bed
9.15	Turns out light	9.30	Turns out light

Maria got up at half past seven this morning and arrived at school at quarter to nine. Her first lesson was History. It is now eleven o'clock. She has just had a break. She is studying English now. The next lesson will be Science. After that there will be a break for lunch. School will end at four o'clock. Maria will get home at half past four. She will go to bed at nine o'clock. She will turn out the light at quarter past nine and will be fast asleep before ten o'clock.

Now write a similar paragraph about Roberto. He goes to a different school, but the time is still eleven o'clock.

This is part of a crossword puzzle:

W		D		E		D	A	Y

There are three blanks here. Put E in the first blank. Put N in the second blank, and put S in the third blank. Then you will make the word WEDNESDAY.

Now write four similar sentences about each of these:

1
S		T	U		D	Y

(a day of the week)

2
L	A		G	U		G	E

(you speak it)

3
S	E	V		N	T		N

(a number)

4
B	L	A		K	B	A		D

(a part of the classroom)

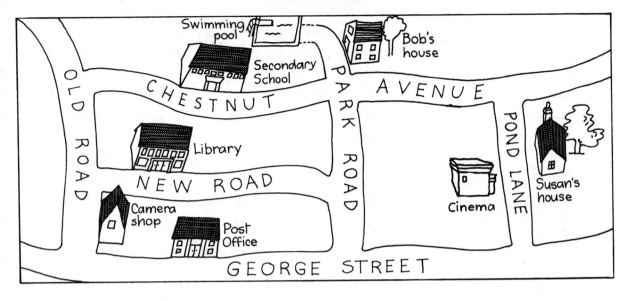

A Copy these. Put in the missing words.

1 When Susan goes to the library, she walks along __ __ to George Street. There she turns right. She walks along George Street for about 100 yards and then turns __ into Park Road. About 50 yards along the road she turns left. She walks nearly to the end of __ __ and finds the library on her __.

2 Bob wanted some stamps yesterday. He ran all the way to the post office. He ran along Park Road and crossed over __ __. He went to the end of __ __ and then turned __ into George Street. He ran another 100 yards and came to the post office on his __.

3 When Susan goes to school tomorrow, she will go up Pond Lane to __ __. There she will turn __ and walk down the Avenue. She will cross over __ __ and continue for about 200 yards. She will come to the school on her __.

B Now finish these:

1 *Bob goes to the library once a week. He walks . . .*
2 *Susan went to the cinema yesterday evening. She . . .*
3 *Bob is going to have a look at the camera shop this afternoon. He will . . .*
4 *Susan walks to school every day. She goes . . .*
5 *Susan is going to have a party tomorrow. Bob will be there. He will . . .*
6 *Susan went to the swimming pool yesterday . . .*

Can you write these sentences in the correct order?

In the middle of a battle at sea his captain said, 'I must send a message to the ship over there, but I cannot put out a boat, because it is not safe.'

This happened in the days of sailing ships.

He said, 'Let me swim there, sir; I can carry the letter in my teeth.'

He reached the other boat, climbed up a rope and gave up his letter.

Shovel was a young cabin boy.

He held the letter in his teeth and swam.

The little boy took off his clothes and jumped into the sea.

Shovel heard this.

Shots fell all round him, but he swam on.

The Captain looked at him and said, 'You can try, boy.'

Now tell the story of the pictures below. The answers to these questions will help you:

Was the diver under the water?
What attacked him?
Did the octopus put its tentacles round his leg?
Who did the diver telephone?
What did he say to the boat above?
Did another diver come down?
What did he come with?
What did he cut?
Did the two divers then swim to the top?

Here are some more riddles:

a It is round, yellow and cold. It shines at night, but it does not shine during the day. Men have already landed on it. What is it?

b This usually has shelves and a door. We sometimes put food in it, and we sometimes put clothes in it. What is it?

c The teacher wrote with a piece of this yesterday. He will write with a piece tomorrow. He often writes with a piece. It is usually white, but it is sometimes yellow, green or red. What is it?

d This is not a thing; it is a person. She will be a woman, but she is not a woman yet. She goes to school. What is she?

e This is another person. He was a boy, but he is not a boy now. He worked in a hospital yesterday. He is working in a hospital today. He will work in a hospital tomorrow. His name begins with D. What is he?

Now write similar riddles about each of these:

1	a pencil	**3**	a boy	**5**	a piece of paper
2	a plane	**4**	a nurse	**6**	a bicycle

TIME	MONDAY
9.00– 9.40	History
9.40–10.20	Maths
10.20–11.00	English
11.00–11.15	Break
11.15–11.55	Science
11.55–12.35	P.E.
12.35– 2.00	Lunch
2.00– 2.40	Maths
2.40– 3.20	Geography
3.20– 4.00	Art

part of Bob's timetable
P.E. = physical education

It is now quarter to ten on Monday morning. Bob has finished his History lesson. He has now begun his Maths lesson. The Maths lesson will finish at twenty past ten. The next lesson will be English. That will finish at eleven o'clock.

Imagine it is:
1 quarter to three
2 five past two
3 twenty-five past ten
4 twenty past eleven

Write seven sentences for each time.

Write the story of the pictures. These questions will help you.

1 The boy in the car is Bob. Did he go to the seaside or to a farm for his holiday?

2 Bob often went to the beach. What did he see one day? What did he think? Did he think: 'Perhaps that ship is going to Holland'?

3 What did he do that evening? Did he put his letter in a bottle? Who did he write the letter to?

4 What did he do with the letter next morning?

5 What happened between picture 4 and picture 6? What country did the bottle go to?

6 Who found the bottle on the beach? Did the Dutch boy read the letter inside the bottle?

7 What did he do after that? Who received the letter from the Dutch boy?

8 What happened after that? How did Bob travel to Holland? Who met the boat?

52

BOB **Think of a double number.**

ANN **OK, I have thought of one.**

BOB **Multiply it by two.**

ANN **Right.**

BOB **Add one.**

ANN **Yes, I've added one.**

BOB **Now multiply by five.**

ANN **I've multiplied by five.**

BOB **Now add five.**

ANN **Yes, I've done that.**

BOB **Finally, multiply by ten and give me the number.**

ANN **The number is 2,200.**

BOB **Then you thought of the number 21.**

ANN **You are right. But how do you know?**

(The answer is always one less than the first two figures of the final number: 22 − 1.)

We can write this puzzle in symbols: $21 \times 2 + 1 \times 5 + 5 \times 10 = 2,200$.

a Now write these sums in words. Begin like this: *Start with the number 12 . . .*

    (a) $12 \times 2 + 1 \times 5 + 5 \times 10 = 1,300$

    (b) $30 \times 2 + 1 \times 5 + 5 \times 10 = 3,100$

    (c) $6 \times 3 + 2 \times 4 + 10 \times 2 = 180$

    (d) $10 + 12 \times 5 + 40 \times 2 = 300$

    (e) $87 + 3 \times 2 + 20 \times 5 = 1,000$

    (f) $60 + 10 - 20 \times 2 + 50 = 150$

b Ann did these sums last week. What did she do? This is what she did with the first one: **She started with the number 13. She took away three. Then she added five. Next she multiplied by two and took away ten. After that she multiplied by five. Finally she added fifty. The answer was a hundred and fifty.**

    (a) $13 - 3 + 5 \times 2 - 10 \times 5 + 50 = 150$

    (b) $10 - 2 + 12 \times 3 - 10 \times 2 + 30 = 130$

    (c) $50 - 20 + 10 \times 2 + 20 = 100$

    (d) $6 \times 4 - 14 + 20 \times 2 - 50 = 10$

    (e) $73 - 13 \times 2 - 20 + 50 \times 2 = 300$

There are eleven players in every football team. The average age of the players in Blank Team was 22. During a game one player injured his leg. He went off the field. The average age of the ten players still on the field was then 21. How old was the injured man?

Explain how you got your answer. Begin: *The total age of the eleven players was . . .*

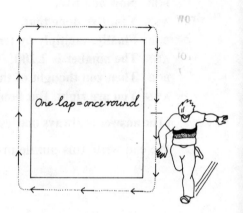

One lap = once round

Bob ran round the garden seven times. The first lap took 60 seconds. The second lap took 70 seconds. He added ten seconds to his time each time he did a lap. How long did the last lap take? Explain how you got your answer. Begin like this: *Bob did five laps after the second one . . .*

Bob had three sandwiches and John had five. Peter didn't have any sandwiches, but he had 8p.

   'Can I share your sandwiches?' Peter asked. 'I will give you 8p.'

   'Yes, we will share our sandwiches with you,' Bob and John said.

   They cut up their sandwiches. Each boy took an equal amount. The three boys ate their lunch.

Then Bob said to John, 'I gave three sandwiches and you gave five. So you must take 5p and I must take 3p. That is fair.'

But was it fair? What was the correct division of money? Write your answer like this:

No, . . . Each of the boys. . . . So John gave Peter . . ., but Bob. . . . Therefore the correct . . .

91

The commentator (20) reported the next day. Write what he said. Begin: *Tom Wilson had the ball. He ran along the left wing . . .*

92

You mended a puncture yesterday. Write down what you did (21). Begin: *First, I turned my bicycle upside-down. Then I . . .*

93

Jill Brown is not living at 21 Park Road yet (42). She is going to live there soon. Rewrite what Jill wrote. Begin like this: *My name is Jill Brown. I am going to live at 21 Park Road. Our neighbours on one side will be the Smiths. . . .*

94

Look at the map (45). Explain to a stranger how he makes these journeys:
a   from the cinema to the police station
b   from the swimming pool to the cinema
c   from the football stadium to the secondary school

95

Look at the map again (45). You made these journeys last week. Write down where you went.
a   from the secondary school to the cinema
b   from the football stadium to the police station
c   from the library to the swimming pool

96

It is 6.30 in the morning. Tom is still asleep (53). Write down what he will do up to 4.30 p.m. Begin: *Tom will wake up at half past seven. He will . . .*

97

Look at the map (81). Give a stranger instructions for these journeys:
a   from Susan's house to the library
b   from the camera shop to Bob's house

98

Write similar sentences about yourself (85). Begin: *It is now . . . I have finished . . .* If you are writing at home, choose an imaginary lesson.

This list gives the new structures practised in each unit. Any structures practised earlier may also be used; they are not listed except where specially heavy practice is offered. Units 1–4 come within Stage One of Longman Structural Readers and units 5–98 all come within Stage Two. All the units come within Book One of A. S. Hornby's *The Teaching of Structural Words and Sentence Patterns* (OUP).

1 Present tense of '*to be*' with prepositional phrases (*in, on, at*).

2 Prepositional phrases with present tense of '*to be*'.

3 *Here are . . . Are these your . . .? Yes, they are. No, they aren't.*

4 *Two and nine are eleven.*

5 Apostrophe *s*; *first, second, third.*

6 *Of* (a picture of) with present tense of '*to be*' only.

7 *Whose car is that? Which one? The one in front of . . .*

8 *I can see some* + prepositional phrase.

9 *He can see some* + prepositional phrase.

10 *I can't see . . .; Where is it?*

11 *Can I . . .? Yes, you can. No, you can't.*

12 *Twice three is six. Fifteen and six are twenty-one.*

13 Present continuous: *He/She is sitting . . . They are watching a . . .*

14 Present continuous: S + V + O; S + V + prepositional phrase.

15 Present continuous; general consolidation.

16 Time (*It is quarter to eight.*) *He is getting up/ putting on . . .*

17 *What is he/she/it/doing? Is he/she/it eating? What is he/she/it eating?*

18 First–sixth; *Where is he going?*

19 Present continuous: S + V + prepositional phrase.

20 Present continuous.

21 Present continuous; the imperative with *First . . . Then . . . Next . . .*

22 *There is . . .*

23 *There are/aren't any . . .*

24 *There are two groups of children in the pictures above.*

25 *There are already . . .; There is someone . . .*

26 *Is there a . . .? What is there . . .?*

27 *Who is there . . .?*

28 *There is something . . .; There is nothing . . .*

29 General consolidation.

30 *Is/Are there . . .? How many are there . . .?*

31 *He has/they have . . .*

32 *He/She has no . . .; I have . . .*

33 *He/She has dark;* present continuous; *I can see . . .*

34 *Budapest has a population of 1,900,000.*

35 Phrasal verbs: *pumping/pulling/sweeping/hanging/up.*

36 Present simple: *She lives/speaks . . .; I live/ speak . . .*

37 *Fourteen plus six equals twenty.*

38 Present simple: S + V(+ O) + prepositional phrase.

39 *Where does . . .? What does . . .?*

40 Present simple: S + V(+ IO) + O.

41 Present simple.

42 *The Cooks live opposite us.*

43 *Where do I . . .?* present simple contrasted with present continuous.

44 Present simple with *because.*

45 *How do I . , .?*

46 Present simple: *There is/are . . .*

47 *Going to* (for the future): *He/She is going to . . .*

48 *He/She is going to . . . Then he/she is going to . . .*

49 *How is he going to . . .?*

50 *He is going to do it with . . .*

51 Past simple: *Did he visit . . .? No, he visited . . . Yes, he did. No, he didn't.*

52 Past simple: S + V + IO + O.

53 Past simple contrasted with present simple; S + V(+ O) + time phrase.

54 Past simple in narrative.

55 Past simple with phrasal verb: *I crossed out . . .*

56 Past simple of '*to have*': *They had three children.*

57 Past simple of '*to be*': *Bob was the goalkeeper.*

58 Past simple with phrasal verb.

59 Past simple in narrative, with more phrasal verbs.